Woozy the Wizard

A Spell to Get Well

For Eve and Jack
who really do work magic
E. W.

For Annie and Casper
A. M.

First published in 2014
by Faber and Faber Limited
Bloomsbury House
74–77 Great Russell Street
London WC1B 3DA

Designed by Faber and Faber
Printed in China

A CIP record for this book is available from the British Library

978-0571-31109-5

FSC
www.fsc.org
MIX
Paper from
responsible sources
FSC® C008047

2 4 6 8 10 9 7 5 3 1

Woozy the Wizard

A Spell to Get Well

by Elli Woollard

Illustrated by Al Murphy

ff

FABER & FABER

In the faraway village
of Snottington Sneeze
Lived a wizened old wizard
with knocketty knees.

Woozy the wizard
had a cloak that was black,
And he lived with his **pig**
in a ramshackle shack.

1

The people loved Woozy –

    when things needed sorting

He'd say a good spell

    (while his pig sat there snorting).

He'd simply go tapetty-tap

    on his hat,

Say, '**Abra-ca-donkey**'

    and that would be that.

Then he'd pick up his pig

and his trusty old broom,

Cry, 'Yipidee-doo!'

and around he would zoom.

3

But one Monday morning

the sun shone down bright,

Yet nothing in Snottington Sneeze

seemed quite right.

'Atchoo!' sniffed the blacksmith.

'Atchoo!' snuffed the weaver.

'Atchoo!' sneezed the baker.

'We're shaking with fever.

'We've colds in our noses

and poor frozen toeses,

'And spots on our bots

that are redder than roses.

'We're crying, we're sighing,

it's terribly tragic.

'Oh **please** make us better,

just give us some magic.'

'Hmm,' said the wizard,

    'this task won't be easy.

'You're spotty and dotty

    and snotty and sneezy.

'But piffles to sniffles,

    I'll soon make you well!

'Let me look in my book

    for a suitable spell.'

Woozy's book was all crinkled

and crusted with crumbs

And ink stains and **think** stains

and smears from his thumbs.

But the wisdom of wizards

from all through the ages

Was written in gold

on those precious pink pages.

So Woozy sat down

    and for hours he just read,

Till the spells pinged liked popcorn

    inside his old head.

He groaned to his pig

    and he scratched at his beard.

'My magic!' he cried.

    'Has it all disappeared?

'I've looked at this book

    for a day and a night

'And I've found lots of spells,

    but they don't seem quite right . . .

'There are spells to cure grumbling

    and spells to cure stumbling

'And spells to cure bees

    who refuse to stop bumbling,

14

'A spell to pull wool from

a bull's hairy tum.

'But **no** spell to get well!'

And he sat feeling glum.

'Then how,' Woozy said,

    'can I warm my friends' toeses,

'And rid them of sneezes

    and spots like red roses?

'. . . Until I can cure

    all the villagers' pox

'I will just have to knit them

    some warm woolly socks!'

Woozy's needles went

clicketty-clicketty-clack

As he knitted in purple

and silver and black . . .

17

18

'Socks!' shouted Woozy.

 'Oh Pig, look at those!

'Now all of my friends will have

 toasty warm toes.'

But the blacksmith went 'sniff',

 and the weaver went 'sneeze'.

The baker said, 'Woozy,

 just do something, please!'

'Oh Pig,' Woozy said,

    'socks are lovely and snug,

'But I'll still need a **spell**

    to get rid of this bug!

'What can I do for

    their noses and toeses

'And spots on their bots

    that are redder than roses?'

Woozy had a good think

and he scratched at his chin.

Then, 'I've got it!' he cheered

with a wide-open grin.

'I'll ask my friend **Dripsy**,

the dragon of Droo,

'She's as smart as jam tarts;

she'll know just what to do.'

So he and his pig

whooshed away on their broom

22

Till they came to the woods,

full of darkness and gloom.

And there, in a lair

   filled with puffs of pink smoke,

A dragon slid out,

   looked around, and then spoke:

24

'My dear old friend, Woozy!

Is something the matter?

'Come and sit down

for a chit-chatty natter.'

So Woozy explained

   that he had to solve sneezing

And spot-dotted bots

   and poor toes that were freezing.

He needed a **spell!**

   So Dripsy said, 'Here.'

And whispered some words

   in his wizened old ear;

A spell that the dragon

had hidden away

To use on a snivelling sneeze

sort of day.

'Thanks, Dripsy!' said Woozy,

'I'll give it a try.'

And he and his pig

shot away through the sky.

'Pig!' laughed the wizard.

'They'll soon all be well!'

But when he got home . . .

He'd FORGOTTEN the spell!

'Oh, Pig,' Woozy sighed,

'I'm a muddly old mess.

'What were the words?

I'll just have to guess!'

'Abracadollop!'

he called in the breeze . . .

But all that he got

were some carrots and peas . . .

And plump lumps of dumpling,

all fluffy and big.

'I've spoiled my spell!'

Woozy said to his pig.

'What can I **do** for

      their noses and toeses

'And spots on their bots

      that are redder than roses?

'Until I remember

      the spell to cure flu

'I will brew them a pot

      of some steaming hot stew.'

'Pig!' Woozy smiled.

    'Fetch my cauldron and stirrer,

'Then get me my apron,

    my whisk and my whirrer.'

And into the cauldron

    went onions and beans,

A pipkin of pepper,

    a sprig of spring greens.

With sploshes and splashes

and **spluttery splishes,**

He spooned all the stew

into bowls and big dishes.

But the weaver went 'sniff',

and the baker went 'sneeze'.

The blacksmith said, 'Woozy,

just do something, please!'

Baffled and bothered,

the wizard came home,

Where he washed up the bowls

in a mountain of foam.

Then he gazed for a while

at his old crystal ball,

Which filled up with fog

and then . . . **nothing at all!**

'Oh, Pig!' Woozy wailed,

    as he started to weep.

'My magic won't work

    when my ball's gone to sleep.

'What can I **do** for

    their noses and toeses

'And spots on their bots

    that are redder than roses?'

'My spells never work,

they're still ill,' Woozy said.

'So I'll tuck them up tight

in a soft snuggly bed.'

A bed full of pillows,

all plumpy and puffy,

And blissful warm blankets,

all fleecy and fluffy.

And squillions of quilts

and a thousand warm throws

To cover their chests

and their poor frozen toes.

But the baker **still** sniffled,

the blacksmith **still** sneezed,

The weaver said, 'Woozy,

just do something, please!'

'My magic!' he moaned

as he slumped out the door.

'It's simply no use

in this place any more.'

Woozy flew with his pig

over lakes and a pond,

Till they came to the hills

in the Back of Beyond . . .

Where Woozy sat down

and said to his pig,

'I'm just a small wizard;

this task is **too big**.'

And he moaned and he groaned

and he droned to himself,

Until out from a hole there popped . . .

Iffy the elf!

'Why, Iffy!' cried Woozy.

'I'm so pleased it's you!

'My friends are all ill.

Tell me, what should I do?'

'Do?' said the elf.

'But your fame has spread far!

'You're a whizz of a wizard!

A wonder! A star!

'Your name's in the papers,

just look at the news:

'All of your friends

are now cured of their flus.

'No colds in their noses

or poor frozen toeses

'Or spots on their bots

that are redder than roses.'

'WHAT . . .?'

Woozy said.

'. . . How are they better,

yes **how** are they well?

'I didn't use magic;

I don't have a spell!'

'But you gave them **thick socks**,'

the wise Iffy said.

'You served them **warm stew**

and you tucked them in **bed**.

'And now they're much better –

it's all thanks to you.

'Your **goodness** is magic,

it's magic, it's true!'

Back in the village

of Snottington Sneeze

Lives a wizened old wizard

with knocketty knees.

Woozy flies through the skies

going zippety zoom

As he and his pig

whoosh around on their broom.

Woozy waves at the blacksmith,

he waves at the weaver,

He waves at the baker,

now cured of the fever.

He loops in the air

and dips down to the ground.

'Woozy,' they call,

'you're the best whizz around!

'Your magic's a muddle

but none of us mind;

'We **love you**, dear wizard,

because you are kind.'